D0777116

PEABODY INSTITUTE LIBRARY
15 SYLVAN STREET
DANVERS, MASSACHUSETTS 01923

MAR 1 7 2009

DEMCO

A Note to Parents

DK READERS is a compelling program for beginning readers, designed in conjunction with leading literacy experts, including Dr. Linda Gambrell, Professor of Education at Clemson University. Dr. Gambrell has served as President of the National Reading Conference and the College Reading Association, and has recently been elected to serve as President of the International Reading Association.

Beautiful illustrations and superb full-color photographs combine with engaging, easy-to-read stories to offer a fresh approach to each subject in the series. Each DK READER is guaranteed to capture a child's interest while developing his or her reading skills, general knowledge, and love of reading.

The five levels of DK READERS are aimed at different reading abilities, enabling you to choose the books that are exactly right for your child:

Pre-level 1: Learning to read
Level 1: Beginning to read
Level 2: Beginning to read alone
Level 3: Reading alone
Level 4: Proficient readers

The "normal" age at which a child begins to read can be anywhere from three to eight years old. Adult participation through the lower levels is very helpful for providing encouragement, discussing storylines, and sounding out unfamiliar words.

No matter which level you select, you can be sure that you are helping your child learn to read, then read to learn!

DK

LONDON, NEW YORK, MUNICH,
MELBOURNE, and DELHI

Editorial Lead Heather Jones
Special Sales Production Manager
Silvia La Greca
Associate Publisher Nigel Duffield

Reading Consultant
Linda Gambrell, Ph.D.

Produced by
Shoreline Publishing Group LLC
President James Buckley, Jr.
Designer Tom Carling, carlingdesign.com

The Boy Scouts of America®, Cub Scouts®,
Boys' Life®, and rank insignia are registered
trademarks of the Boy Scouts of America.
Printed under license from the
Boy Scouts of America.

First American Edition, 2008
08 09 10 11 10 9 8 7 6 5 4 3 2 1
Published in the United States by DK Publishing
375 Hudson Street, New York, New York 10014

Copyright © 2008 Dorling Kindersley Limited

All rights reserved under International and Pan-American
Copyright Conventions. No part of this publication may be
reproduced, stored in a retrieval system, or transmitted in any form
or by any means, electronic, mechanical, photocopying, recording,
or otherwise, without the prior written permission of
the copyright owner.

Published in Great Britain by Dorling Kindersley Limited

DK books are available at special discounts when purchased in bulk
for sales promotions, premiums, fund-raising, or educational use.
For details, contact:
DK Publishing Special Markets, 375 Hudson St., New York, NY 10014
SpecialSales@dk.com

A catalog record for this book is available
from the Library of Congress.
ISBN: 978-0756-637170 (Paperback)

Printed and bound in China by L. Rex Printing Co. Ltd.

Special thanks to Brian, Brandon, Daniel, and Conor
for their time in the woods!

The publisher would like to thank the following for their kind
permission to reproduce their photographs:
(Key: a=above; b=below/bottom; c=center; l=left; r=right; t=top)
AP/Wide World: 17, 45; Ralph Clevenger: 18; Dreamstime.com (photographers
listed): Zygis41 8, Alexsandr Lobanov 16; Ljupco Smokovski 27, Duncan Gilbert
28b; Mike Eliason: 5, 14, 15, 31, 32-41, 44; iStock: 7, 9, 25; 28t, 43;
Courtesy Garmin Co.: 12; Photos.com: 26, 29.
All other images © Dorling Kindersley Limited.
For more information see: www.dkimages.com

Discover more at

www.dk.com

Contents

DK READERS

READING
3
ALONE

Boys' Life SERIES

Let's Go

Geocaching

Written by John McKinney

PEABODY INSTITUTE
LIBRARY
DANVERS, MASS.

DK
DK Publishing

What is geocaching?

As you hike along the meadow's edge, you check your GPS device: 0.5m, half-mile to go. There's treasure to be found.

300 feet. You cross a stream, and on the other side you spot a metal gate and an old barn. The treasure could be in a magnetic box stuck to the metal gate. Or hidden inside the barn.

120 feet. Not the barn, so it must be the gate. You hurry closer.

150 feet. Oops, wrong way.

You read the clue again: "Where fire came from the sky."

You look around. You see an old oak tree. Its trunk is blackened and split. Did a lightning bolt hit it? The fire from the sky! You hurry toward it.

50 feet, 20 feet, 10 feet . . . bingo! You find the treasure box in a hollow in the tree! Congratulations, you've just been "geocaching."

Geocaching (pronounced JEE-oh-cashing) is a fun, low-cost way for kids to enjoy the outdoors, get some exercise, and use the latest technology.

With a GPS (Global Positioning System) receiver, you seek out or hide caches. A cache (CASH) is a small container that holds a logbook for you to sign, plus some trinkets and souvenirs.

"Geo" comes from the Greek word meaning "earth." A cache is a place for hiding something. Long ago, explorers, gold miners, and pirates hid things in caches. Your computer has memory hidden in an electronic "cache."

Handheld GPS receiver

Geocaching goes great with hiking, biking, and camping trips. Some caches are just a short walk from a parking lot.

The cache is the small black box at the center.

For other caches, you need to take a hike to reach them.

Geocachers find cache coordinates (longitude and latitude) on Web sites. Enter the coordinates on your GPS receiver, and then follow the directions to the cache. You combine the information from the GPS with clues provided by the person who hid the cache.

Prime Meridian: 0° longitude

Equator: 0° latitude

Orienteering and letterboxing were similar activities before the GPS receivers were invented. Many people still enjoy those games today.

The goal of orienteering is to get from one point to another using a map and a compass. Orienteering offers a great outdoors experience and requires lots of thinking and concentration.

It can be done for fun with a group of friends or as a competition.

Letterboxing is a mixture of treasure-hunting, hiking, and arts and crafts. You follow clues to locate a small box hidden somewhere outdoors. A typical letterbox holds a notebook, a unique rubber stamp, and an inkpad. Finders can stamp their notebooks to show they've found that letterbox. However, you don't get to use a GPS!

Letterboxing got started in England about 150 years ago and came to the United States in the late 1990s.

Mr. Geocache

In 2000, when GPS devices were first sold to the public, Dave Ulmer of Oregon started hiding what he first called "stashes." His hobby became geocaching.

GPS receivers in action

Geocaching works thanks to two dozen satellites orbiting the Earth, plus some ground stations. When you use your GPS outdoors, it receives radio signals from four of the satellites. After gathering signals from the satellites, the GPS calculates your location anywhere on the planet. It tells your exact position in latitude and longitude coordinates.

Even if you're hiking in a thick fog, on a moonless night, or in a snowstorm, a GPS receiver will plot your exact location anytime, anywhere.

So does a GPS replace a map and compass?

No, it does not. Remember that a GPS unit, like a compass, is just a navigation tool. Having a GPS on a hike or during a geocaching expedition certainly is not a substitute for common sense and paying attention to where you're going.

Also, a GPS receiver is only a receiver and cannot broadcast a signal. So you don't have to worry about space aliens tracking you. However, remember that you also can't depend on it helping others find you if you get lost!

Typical GPS receiver

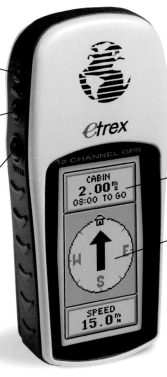

Up: scrolls up the map

Down: scrolls down the map

Enter/Mark: Push to put a location into the GPS memory

Power button is on right side

Distance to cache

Direction to go toward cache; can also show map and waypoints

You can buy a good handheld GPS for about $100. Look in electronic stores, sporting good stores, or online.

A good GPS receiver should be compact, waterproof, and rugged. Make sure it has software installed to help you plan, follow, and record a route.

For most types of geocaching, you probably don't need the "extras," or the fancy range of features offered by high-cost receivers.

However, if you're going to use your GPS in remote areas, consider getting a more advanced unit. It will have more memory and a computer connection to download maps. Some GPS devices can also display topographic maps and other detailed maps.

Basic Features of a GPS
- Waterproof
- Long battery life
- Strong reception (so that you won't lose the signal in canyon bottoms or thick forests)
- Storage of at least 20 routes (that means the GPS will remember up to 20 different cache paths)
- Storage of at least 500 waypoints. A waypoint is like an electronic trail marker; they let you know that you're on the right path. You can enter them youself as you go along, too.

The main purpose of a GPS is to keep you on course as you move toward your destination. Some receivers also show how far you've traveled.

This closeup shows how the GPS shows you where to go.

The best way to learn to use a GPS receiver is by going out in the field with an experienced user. Every model is different, so try to learn to use your own receiver.

It won't take you very long to learn enough about your GPS to go geocaching. You'll soon be able to enter coordinates and waypoints and use them to plan your route. Waypoints show electronically the steps you need to take along the route to the cache.

After finding a cache, the GPS helps create a record of your search. That way, you can share the site and route of that cache with friends or plan a future outing on the same trail.

The treasure you seek

Geocachers get two rewards: the joy of finding the cache and the fun of hiking with friends.

The caches themselves are waterproof containers holding a logbook. In the logbook, you can record your name and the date and other thoughts about your hike. Logbooks sometimes reveal the coordinates of other caches; they can be pretty funny, too!

The logbook may be a good-sized notebook or a tightly rolled slip of paper. Some geocaches also have a small camera so visitors can snap pictures of themselves at the cache site.

Discovery! Finding a cache after a hike is a real treat.

Many caches have treasures, also known as prizes, trinkets, or "swag" (short for "stuff we all get"). Remember the geocache treasure rule: If you take a treasure, you must leave something of equal or greater value. So bring some small things with you to "trade." There's a list of ideas on page 20.

The Travel Bug

KZZNNY

Do not keep me!
I am a Travel Bug
Help me travel from
cache to cache
Visit
www.groundspeak.com
to learn about me
and how to help me on
my next adventure

Groundspeak

One of the fun things to buy online—
or create—is a Travel Bug, an item
with a numbered dog-tag attached to
it. A Travel Bug "visits" places all over
the world, thanks to helpful humans
like you. If you find one, help the Bug
along its journey by taking a photo of

it, logging its new visit on its Web page (the dog tag usually has the address), and leaving it in another cache somewhere else. To make your own Travel Bug, attach one of the dog tags to your Bug. Keep a duplicate tag as a reminder of the i.d. number.

In all cases of treasure, practice the Geocaching Golden Rule: Leave for others what you'd like others to leave for you.

Also, when you find a cache and there are non-geocachers around, examine it and put it back in its hiding place without the "geomuggles" noticing. People who geocache refer to those who don't as "muggles"—a word from the Harry Potter books meaning a person without magical powers.

Cache Contents

Take the time to purchase or make fun, interesting, tradable items. You can find special geocaching coins and pins, or use your imagination. Here are a few suggestions for "treasures":

- Visit a "dollar store" to look for small toys: cars, bouncy balls, penlights, costume jewelry, a kazoo.
- Your local outdoor world can be a good place to find "nature treasures," such as as polished stones, unusual sea shells, pretty feathers, or small crystals.
- Homemade pins, lanyards, bracelets, or key chains.
- Outdoor gear, because geocachers love the outdoors and appreciate things like carabiners (metal clips) and emergency rain coats.
- Identity items such as wooden or metal "geocoins" or patches given by members of clubs or organizations.

Here's what NOT to leave:
- Broken toys are trash, not treasures.
- Dangerous objects such as matches or firecrackers. If you can't take it to school, don't leave it in a geocache.
- Food: Animals will sniff out the food and get into the cache.
- Trash: You'd think everyone would know better than to leave soda cans,

candy wrappers, and other litter in a cache!

- Rocks and pine cones found nearby.
- Advertisements: Adults sometimes leave behind flyers about their businesses, but they shouldn't. No commercials!

Types of Caches

- A microcache is a very small cache, the size of a film canister or magnetic key holder.
- A small cache is larger than a micro. You might use one of small tins that some mints come in.
- A standard or regular cache uses a plastic food container (left) or larger, metal can.
- A large cache can be as big as a five-gallon bucket!
- Multi-caches have two or more finds, each with clues directing you to a treasure.
- A virtual cache is just a place without a hidden object. It's often somewhere with a special natural beauty or historical landmark. The description you provide proves you were there.
- A Webcam cache is pretty neat. The coordinates send you to a public Webcam such as in a park entrance or on a bridge. Then the Webcam takes your picture to record your "find."

Tracking down the caches

Your geocaching adventure begins on the Internet. Check with your parents, and then go online to www.geocaching. com. This site features thousands of geocaches and their coordinates. You'll need to register in order to log on and search for a cache near you.

Before registering, think up a code name for yourself. Geocachers like to use made-up names like "MadDog" or "Cache-Buster" instead of real names. You also need to know your home zip code and the coordinates of your home. Use a GPS to find home coordinates.

Search for cache locations by country, state, and zip code. If the location is in a nature park or wild place, find the name of the nearest town.

Get started by entering your home zip code. Look for listings of geocaches nearby. Results will be listed on the site from nearest to farthest away.

The names of geocaches are often amusing, such as Walk the Plank, Beware of Frogs, or Smokey Bear's Treasures. Choose a geocache site that is near you and sounds interesting.

A sample page from geocaching.com

Note to Parents: Web sites such as the one mentioned here are not endorsed by Boy Scouts of America or DK Publishing and have not been completely examined. However, at press time, they provided the sort of information described. Internet experts always suggest that you work with your children to help them understand how to safely navigate the Web.

Then look for the coordinates of the cache. That's the most important thing. Every spot on the Earth can be named by these coordinates. Here's one for a cache in Morro Bay, California:

Latitude is noted in North or South; in this case it's North.

This number is read in "minutes."

This number is read in "seconds."

N 35° 20.709

W 120° 50.623

Longitude is shown as East or West; here, the location is West.

The longitude and latitude are measured in "degrees," which translate into distance from the 0° line (longitude) in England or the Equator (latitude).

Those numbers match up to the longitude and latitude of that spot. You'll enter those numbers on your GPS so it can lead you to the cache.

The cache listing will also tell you the size of the cache and when it was placed. You'll also find out how far away the cache is from you.

Each cache is listed with degrees of difficulty and terrain. When choosing a cache, pay close attention to the difficulty ratings. Geocaches are rated by a five-star system (from one for easy to five for difficult) according to how well they're hidden. A second five-star rating tells you the difficulty of the terrain you'll have to cross.

Counting finders

On the cache listing page, you might see a "log count." This shows how many people have found the cache (happy faces) and the number of people who didn't (frowning faces). An online logbook might also have comments about the cache.

Start by looking for caches rated one or two stars in both categories. A one-star cache with parking nearby is known by geocachers as a "Drive-by," "Park and Grab," or "Cache and Dash."

Most cache listings have maps that help you locate where the search begins. Finding the starting point of your adventure can be part of the fun.

Also, finding caches is not just digital: There are important clues you have to decode before you hit the trail. Look in the "Additional Hints" section of each cache description. There you'll find a clue to the location of the cache. But it's not that easy! Often, the clues are listed in the form of a code, riddle, or puzzle.

Decode this clue

Match up letters using the key below to decode this clue. The clue will help a geocacher find the cache.

Haqre n ohfu naq oruvaq n ebpx

Decryption Key:

```
N O P Q R C G U V J X L K A B Y D E F T H S W Z I M
A B C D E F G H I J K L M N O P Q R S T U V W X Y Z
```

Answer: "Under a bush and behind a rock."

In the field

One of the best parts of geocaching is getting out into nature. As you hike the trail toward a geocache, take the time to appreciate the plants, animals, and beauty around you.

What birds can you see? What birds can you hear? Look for hummingbirds drinking nectar, woodpeckers rat-tat-tatting, or hawks circling high overhead. Listen for songbirds singing in the woods and in the brush. Look up at the sky.

It's fun to find shapes in the clouds: a rabbit, an old man, a dragon, a car.

Watch for wildlife: a squirrel racing up a tree trunk, a lizard doing push-ups on a rock, a gopher popping its head above ground.

Imagine how many animals are out there hidden from view. Look for signs of them in the form of tracks, scat (animal poop), or chewed branches.

Outdoor Gear

Along with your GPS receiver, treasures to exchange, and printouts of your coordinates and clues, here are some other things to take along. (Remember, always hike with adults):

- Hiking gear: Bring a day pack that holds water, snacks, dry clothing, and sunscreen.
- Hiking shoes or boots.
- A map of the area: Remember, your GPS might not be enough.
- Compass: Ditto!

> **The Geocachers' Creed**
> When placing or seeking geocaches, I will:
> - Not endanger myself or others.
> - Observe all laws and rules of the area.
> - Respect property rights and seek permission if needed.
> - Avoid causing disruptions.
> - Minimize my impact on the environment.
> - Be considerate of others and animals.
> - Preserve and care for others' caches.

Always plan ahead and prepare, so that you know where you're going and that the weather is safe to travel in. Always travel or camp in safe places. Respect wildlife and be considerate of other hikers and visitors.

Whether geocaching or just hiking, always treat nature with respect and help preserve it. Don't put your hand where you eyes can't see. A cache site might be a home for a snake or spider. Gently use a stick to look for the hidden treasure.

One special way that geocachers respect nature is to always remove any litter. In fact, their rule is "cache in, trash out." While geocaching, take a small bag with you and carry back out out any trash you find.

Let's go geocaching

To learn more about geocaching, let's "go" on a geocaching expedition. We'll follow Brandon, Conor, and Daniel step-by-step as they track and find a geocache near their home in Santa Barbara, California.

First, they meet their scout leader Mr. Gordon at the head of a trail to the cache. They each enter the cache coordinates into their GPS receivers.

When they leave the parking area, they mark its location as a waypoint. A waypoint is a stop along the way. It sounds silly, but when you're working hard to find your way to the cache, you can lose your sense of direction! The waypoints guide you back.

They look at a map to get an idea of the terrain. The GPS only tells direction "as the crow flies," or, in a straight line. But geocachers

On the next few pages, look for these GPS receivers to "count down" the distance to the cache. Here it's 0.41 miles.

are not crows! Most trails don't take a straight line to the geocache, so having a map of the trail is important.

The boys start up the trail, keeping an eye out for any creatures or interesting views. They also

keep a close eye on their GPS receivers as they get closer to the cache.

Suddenly, they lose the signal! As they walk beneath a thick stand of oak trees, the GPS reads: "Weak signal. Need clear view of sky."

Brandon remembers that the GPS needs to "see" the sky (that's where the satellites are, right?). The boys climb a nearby hill to get out from under the trees. Soon, their receivers all get a signal and the hunt is on again.

Then . . . more trouble! As they stand in one place while they stop for a drink,

their receivers all start giving different distance readings, one after another. Very strange!

Then Conor remembers: A GPS responds to movement and constantly changes. If the GPS could speak, it would say: "Don't just stand there— move!" The boys start moving and the signals come back.

On they go, up the trail, shady in places, sunny in others. Meanwhile, the GPS guides them closer and closer.

A GPS displays distance in tenths and hundredths of a mile. For example, 2.10 is two and one-tenth miles. When the geocachers get a reading of 0.19, they get excited. That means they are less than two-tenths of a mile from the geocache. Good thing the boys were paying attention in math class on "decimal day"!

When they get within 0.1 (one-tenth of a mile), the GPS changes its readings and starts counting down in feet instead. They watch as the numbers get lower and lower—500, 428, 260…

However, geocachers know the last 100 feet are always the hardest. A GPS helps put you near a cache, but finding a well-hidden one is a challenge. One trick is to try and think like the person who hid it. Up high? Down low? This is when to use the clues from the Web site.

The boys know they are near, so they start searching high and low. Then Daniel calls out, "I found it!" After using a stick to make sure the hole is safe, he reaches in and pulls out a small cache. Time for high fives all around! Even though the GPS coordinates were very accurate, the cache was still hard to find.

After checking around to make sure there are no nearby geomuggles (people who are not geocachers), the boys open the container and check out the contents of the cache.

Cool stuff! They each take a sticker for their geocache logbooks at home. Each boy also puts in a "treasure" he has brought with him.

They also read the logbook to see who's been there before them. After putting their own names in the logbook, they close the cache back up.

Brandon is careful to put the cache back exactly the way it was found. The boys want the next geocachers who come along to have the same feeling of discovery that they did.

On the way back, they talk about the hunt and where they'll go on their next adventure. Maybe they'll look for a cache that's even harder to find and even farther away. Or maybe they'll head out to plant their own caches.

When they get home, they'll e-mail the person who hid the cache to report that they found it. They'll let them know that the cache was in good condition, and they had a great time finding it!

Do it yourself

Now that you've learned how to find a cache, it's time to place your own.

A cache location shows the skill of the person who hid it—so make the hunt for your cache fun! On a hike with an adult, place the cache in a special place, perhaps where there is a great view or a neat historic site.

Start out by making two decisions:

- Will your cache be easy or difficult to reach? Do you want to hide it in a wilderness area off the trail or by an easy-to-reach pond?
- Will your cache be easy or difficult to find? Do you want to make it a difficult challenge for expert geocachers, or easy enough for kids and families to locate?

Of course, make sure you know who owns the land and its rules about placing caches. Be sure to always ask permission of the landowner if it is not public land.

To create your cache, use a
waterproof container and put important
items like the logbook in plastic bags.
Mark the top of the container as
a "Geocache." Remember, you are
responsible for your cache and for taking
care of the environment around it.

Get the coordinates for your cache site from your GPS. Then come up with a name, description, and clues. If it's okay with your parents, list your cache on a geocaching Web site.

Make sure to visit your cache from time to time to see how many people have signed the logbook . . . and to see what treasures people have added!

Geocaching can be a fun activity if you like a treasure hunt and enjoy being outdoors. You test yourself, and you can play it with other geocachers. And what a terrific feeling it is to be the first to find a cache!

Find out more

Books

The Essential Guide to Geocaching
by Mike Dyer
A book that spotlights the fun of hiking while also giving the basics of geocaching, turning a hike into a treasure hunt.

The Complete Idiot's Guide to Geocaching
by Jack W. Peters
A step-by-step primer on everything from reviews of GPS receivers to the dos and don'ts of building your own caches.

Web sites

The No. 1 site
www.geocaching.com
Your one-stop shopping spot for everything about this fun hobby. Find caches in your area, find out how to list your own caches, and see photos of caches other people have found. This is an awesome reference site.

More than just caches
www.gpsgames.org
This site has caches around the world, as well as games like GeoGolf and ShutterSpot, which add other elements to using your GPS on hikes.

Find out the local rules
www.geocachingpolicy.org
This site lists local and national rules regarding various geocaching and hiking places.

Do the right thing
www.geocreed.info/
This site features a set of guidelines, including "The Geocachers' Creed," for placing and hiding geocaches.

Note to Parents: These Web sites are not endorsed by Boy Scouts of America or DK Publishing and have not been completely examined. However, at press time, they provided the sort of information described. Internet experts always suggest that you work with your children to help them understand how to safely navigate the Web.

Glossary

Cache
[CASH] a hidden container holding a logbook and small trinkets or treasures.

Compact
Made smaller so as to be easily carried or packed.

Concentration
The ability to focus one's attention for a long period of time.

Coordinates
Numbers or letters used to show the location of a certain point or place.

Disruptions
Things that get in the way or cause a bother.

GPS
Global Positioning System, a system of satellites that work with a receiver to locate your exact position anywhere on Earth.

Latitude
A location measurement that relates to horizontal lines beginning at the Equator.

Letterboxing
A treasure-hunting game like geocaching, but using a series of clues rather than a GPS to find hidden containers.

Logbook
a notepad on which a cache finder writes a name, date, and brief description.

Longitude
A location measurement that relates to vertical lines beginning at the Prime Meridian or 0 degrees.

Muggle
A word taken from the popular Harry Potter books, it means a person who is not a geocacher; also geomuggle.

Orienteering
A game or contest that involves locating and hiking to a certain point, using only a map and a compass.

Scat
A general term for animal fecal waste found in the wild.

Terrain
The general look or content of an area of ground, usually relating to its elevation.

Topographic map
A type of map that shows the elevations of a place.

Unique
One of a kind.

Waypoint
A specific place along your route, the coordinates of which are entered into a GPS receiver to track your trail or your progress.

Index